Light Cooking

MEXICAN

PUBLICATIONS INTERNATIONAL, LTD.

Food Guide Pyramid source: U.S. Department of Agriculture/U.S. Department of Health and Human Services.

Recipe Development: Pamela Eimers
Nutritional Analysis: Linda R. Yoakam, M.S., R.D.

Photography: Silver Lining Graphics Inc., Chicago

Pictured on the front cover: Fajitas *(page 48)*.
Pictured on the inside front cover: Green Pea Guacamole with Avocado and Tomato *(page 10)* and Baked Tortilla Chips *(page 12)*.
Pictured on the inside back cover: Tostadas *(page 46)*.
Pictured on the back cover *(from top to bottom)*: Seafood Tacos with Fruit Salsa *(page 38)*, Gazpacho *(page 26)*, Spinach Salad with Orange-Chile Glazed Shrimp *(page 30)* and Bean & Vegetable Burritos *(page 56)*.

ISBN: 0-7853-0780-X

Manufactured in U.S.A.

8   7   6   5   4   3   2   1

Microwave Cooking: Microwave ovens vary in wattage. The microwave cooking times given in this publication are approximate. Use the cooking times as guidelines and check for doneness before adding more time. Consult manufacturer's instructions for suitable microwave-safe cooking dishes.

CONTENTS

Lessons in Smart Eating _____ 6

Appetizers _____ 10

Soups & Salads _____ 22

Tortilla Dishes _____ 38

Main Dishes _____ 66

Nutrition Reference Chart _____ 92

Index _____ 93

Metric Chart _____ 94

LESSONS IN SMART EATING

Today, people everywhere are more aware than ever before about the importance of maintaining a healthful lifestyle. In addition to proper exercise, this includes eating foods that are lower in fat, sodium and cholesterol. The goal of *Light Cooking* is to provide today's cook with easy-to-prepare recipes that taste great, yet easily fit into your dietary goals. Eating well is a matter of making smarter choices about the foods you eat. Preparing the recipes in *Light Cooking* is your first step toward making smart choices a delicious reality.

A Balanced Diet

The U.S. Department of Agriculture and the Department of Health and Human Services have developed a Food Guide Pyramid to illustrate how easy it is to eat a healthier diet. It is not a rigid prescription, but rather a general guide that lets you choose a healthful diet that's right for you. It calls for eating a wide variety of foods to get the nutrients you need and, at the same time, the right amount of calories to maintain a healthy weight.

Food Guide Pyramid
A Guide to Daily Food Choices

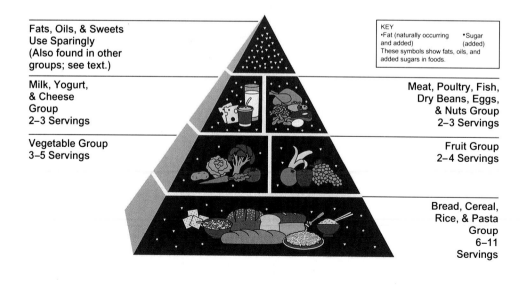

Fats, Oils, & Sweets
Use Sparingly
(Also found in other
groups; see text.)

Milk, Yogurt,
& Cheese
Group
2–3 Servings

Vegetable Group
3–5 Servings

KEY
•Fat (naturally occurring ▼Sugar
and added) (added)
These symbols show fats, oils, and
added sugars in foods.

Meat, Poultry, Fish,
Dry Beans, Eggs,
& Nuts Group
2–3 Servings

Fruit Group
2–4 Servings

Bread, Cereal,
Rice, & Pasta
Group
6–11
Servings

The number of servings, and consequently, the number of calories a person can eat each day, is determined by a number of factors, including age, weight, height, activity level and gender. Sedentary women and some older adults need about 1,600 calories each day. For most children, teenage girls, active women and many sedentary men 2,000 calories is about right. Teenage boys, active men and some very active women use about 2,800 calories each day. Use the chart below to determine how many servings you need for your calorie level.

Personalized Food Group Servings for Different Calorie Levels*			
	1,600	2,000	2,800
Bread Group Servings	6	8	11
Vegetable Group Servings	3	4	5
Fruit Group Servings	2	3	4
Milk Group Servings	2–3**	2–3**	2–3**
Meat Group Servings (ounces)	5	6	7

   * Numbers may be rounded.
  ** Women who are pregnant or breast-feeding, teenagers and young adults to age 24
      need 3 or more servings.

Lower Fat for Healthier Living

It is widely known that most Americans' diets are too high in fat. A low fat diet reduces your risk of getting certain diseases and helps you maintain a healthy weight. Studies have shown that eating more than the recommended amount of fat (especially saturated fat) is associated with increased blood cholesterol levels in some adults. A high blood cholesterol level is associated with increased risk for heart disease. A high fat diet may also increase your chances for obesity and some types of cancer.

Nutrition experts recommend diets that contain 30% or less of total daily calories from fat. The "30% calories from fat" goal applies to a total diet over time, not to a single food, serving of a recipe or meal. To find the approximate percentage of calories from fat use this easy 3-step process:

1 Multiply the grams of fat per serving by 9 (there are 9 calories in each gram of fat), to give you the number of calories from fat per serving.

2 Divide by the total number of calories per serving.

3 Multiply by 100%.

For example, imagine a 200 calorie sandwich that has 10 grams of fat.
To find the percentage of calories from fat, first multiply the grams of fat by 9: $10 \times 9 = 90$

Then, divide by the total number of calories in a serving: $90 \div 200 = .45$

Multiply by 100% to get the percentage of calories from fat: $45 \times 100\% = 45\%$

You may find doing all this math tiresome, so an easier way to keep track of the fat in your diet is to calculate the total *grams* of fat appropriate to your caloric intake, then keep a running count of fat grams over the course of a day. The Nutrition Reference Chart on page 92 lists recommended daily fat intakes based on calorie level.

Defining "Fat Free"

It is important to take the time to read food labels carefully. For example, you'll find many food products on the grocery store shelves making claims such as "97% fat free." This does not necessarily mean that 97% of the *calories* are free from fat (or that only 3 percent of calories come from fat). Often these numbers are calculated by weight. This means that out of 100 grams of this food, 3 grams are fat. Depending on what else is in the food, the percentage of calories from fat can be quite high. You may find that the percent of calories *from fat* can be as high as 50%.

Daily Values

Fat has become the focus of many diets and eating plans. This is because most Americans' diets are too high in fat. However, there are other important nutrients to be aware of, including saturated fat, sodium, cholesterol, protein, carbohydrates and several vitamins and minerals. Daily values for these nutrients have been established by the government and reflect current nutritional recommendations for a 2,000 calorie reference diet. They are appropriate for most adults and children (age 4 or older) and provide excellent guidelines for an overall healthy diet. The chart on page 92 gives the daily values for 11 different items.

Nutritional Analysis

Every recipe in *Light Cooking* is followed by a nutritional analysis block that lists certain nutrient values for a single serving.

■   The analysis of each recipe includes all the ingredients that are listed in that recipe, *except* ingredients labeled as "optional" or "for garnish."

■   If a range is given in the yield of a recipe ("Makes 6 to 8 servings" for example), the *lower* yield was used to calculate the per serving information.

■ If a range is offered for an ingredient ("¼ to ⅛ teaspoon" for example), the *first* amount given was used to calculate the nutrition information.

■ If an ingredient is presented with an option ("2 cups hot cooked rice or noodles" for example), the *first* item listed was used to calculate the nutritional information.

■ Foods shown in photographs on the same serving plate and offered as "serve with" suggestions at the end of a recipe are *not* included in the recipe analysis unless they are listed in the ingredient list.

■ Meat should be trimmed of all visible fat since this is reflected in the nutritional analysis.

■ In recipes calling for cooked rice or noodles, the analysis was based on rice or noodles that were prepared without added salt or fat unless otherwise mentioned in the recipe.

The nutrition information that appears with each recipe was calculated by an independent nutrition consulting firm. Every effort has been made to check the accuracy of these numbers. However, because numerous variables account for a wide range of values in certain foods, all analyses that appear in this book should be considered approximate.

The recipes in this publication are *not* intended as a medically therapeutic program, nor as a substitute for medically approved diet plans for people on fat, cholesterol or sodium restricted diets. You should consult your physician before beginning any diet plan. The recipes offered here can be a part of a healthy lifestyle that meets recognized dietary guidelines. A healthy lifestyle includes not only eating a balanced diet, but engaging in proper exercise as well.

All the ingredients called for in these recipes are generally available in large supermarkets, so there is no need to go to specialty or health food stores. You'll also see an ever-increasing amount of reduced fat and nonfat products available in local markets. Take advantage of these items to reduce your daily fat intake even more.

Cooking Healthier

When cooking great-tasting low fat meals, you will find some techniques or ingredients are different from traditional cooking. Fat serves as a flavor enhancer and gives foods a distinctive and desirable texture. In order to compensate for the lack of fat and still give great-tasting results, many of the *Light Cooking* recipes call for a selection of herbs or a combination of fresh vegetables. A wide variety of grains and pastas are also used. Many of the recipes call for alternative protein sources, such as dried beans or tofu. Often meat is included in a recipe as an accent flavor rather than the star attraction. Vegetables are often "sautéed" in a small amount of broth rather than oil. Applesauce may be added to baked goods to give a texture similar to full fat foods. These are all simple changes that you can easily make when you start cooking healthy!

APPETIZERS

GREEN PEA GUACAMOLE WITH AVOCADO AND TOMATO

❖

If you simply cannot get by without the smooth rich taste of the real McCoy, savor the avocado's flavor in a few chunks. Though most of the avocado's calories come from fat, it is primarily monounsaturated (the kind not associated with heart disease) and contains no cholesterol. So enjoy those tender morsels!

❖

½ cup diced ripe California avocado*
3 tablespoons lemon juice, divided
1 package (16 ounces) frozen petit peas, thawed
4 green onions
½ cup lightly packed fresh cilantro
1 jalapeño pepper, seeded
1 medium tomato, diced
    Baked Tortilla Chips (page 12) (optional)

1 Combine avocado and 1 tablespoon lemon juice in medium bowl.

2 Combine peas, onions, cilantro, remaining 2 tablespoons lemon juice and jalapeño in food processor or blender; process until smooth. Add avocado and tomato; gently stir to combine. Garnish with cilantro or tomato wedges, if desired. Serve with Baked Tortilla Chips (pictured on page 11), if desired.
Makes 8 servings

*To lower fat content, omit avocado.

Nutrients per serving:

Calories	100
(28% of calories from fat)	
Total Fat	3 g
Saturated Fat	1 g
Cholesterol	0 mg
Sodium	141 mg
Carbohydrate	15 g
Dietary Fiber	4 g
Protein	5 g
Calcium	32 mg
Iron	2 mg
Vitamin A	124 RE
Vitamin C	23 mg

DIETARY EXCHANGES:
1 Starch/Bread, ½ Fat

BAKED TORTILLA CHIPS

BAKED FLOUR OR CORN TORTILLA CHIPS

6 (7- to 8-inch) flour tortillas *or* 6 (6-inch) corn tortillas
Paprika, chili powder *or* cayenne pepper

1 Preheat oven to 375°F. Sprinkle 1 tortilla with water to dampen; shake off excess water. Lightly sprinkle top with paprika. Repeat with remaining tortillas. Cut each flour tortilla into 8 wedges, each corn tortilla into 6 wedges.

2 Arrange as many wedges as fit in single layer on baking sheet (edges may overlap slightly). Bake 4 minutes. Rotate sheet. Bake another 2 to 4 minutes until chips are firm and flour tortillas are spotted with light golden color. Do not let corn tortillas brown. Remove chips to plate to cool. Repeat with remaining wedges.

Makes 6 servings

PARMESAN CHIPS

1 Prepare Baked Tortilla Chips as directed above, omitting paprika. Sprinkle each tortilla with 1 tablespoon grated Parmesan cheese and ¼ teaspoon dried oregano leaves.

Makes 6 servings

Nutrients per serving:

*Baked Flour or
Corn Tortilla Chips*

Calories	67
(15% of calories from fat)	
Total Fat	1 g
Saturated Fat	<1 g
Cholesterol	0 mg
Sodium	53 mg
Carbohydrate	13 g
Dietary Fiber	2 g
Protein	2 g
Calcium	42 mg
Iron	<1 mg
Vitamin A	5 RE
Vitamin C	0 mg

DIETARY EXCHANGES:
1 Starch/Bread

Nutrients per serving:

Parmesan Chips

Calories	97
(28% of calories from fat)	
Total Fat	3 g
Saturated Fat	1 g
Cholesterol	5 mg
Sodium	170 mg
Carbohydrate	13 g
Dietary Fiber	2 g
Protein	5 g
Calcium	134 mg
Iron	1 mg
Vitamin A	21 RE
Vitamin C	0 mg

DIETARY EXCHANGES:
1 Starch/Bread, ½ Fat

(continued on page 13)

Baked Tortilla Chips, continued

Nutrients per serving:

Sweet Tortilla, Cinnamon-Sugar or *Fiery Sweet Chips*

Calories	118
(22% of calories from fat)	
Total Fat	3 g
Saturated Fat	<1 g
Cholesterol	0 mg
Sodium	78 mg
Carbohydrate	22 g
Dietary Fiber	2 g
Protein	2 g
Calcium	50 mg
Iron	1 mg
Vitamin A	28 RE
Vitamin C	0 mg

DIETARY EXCHANGES:
1 Starch/Bread, ½ Fruit, ½ Fat

SWEET TORTILLA CHIPS

    1 tablespoon margarine
1½ teaspoons water
¼ cup firmly packed brown sugar
    6 (6- to 7-inch) flour tortillas

1 Microwave margarine and water at HIGH (100% power) in small microwavable bowl for 15 seconds or until margarine melts. Stir in brown sugar until smooth.

2 Spread equal amount of sugar mixture over top of each tortilla, leaving ½-inch border. Cut as directed for Baked Flour Tortilla Chips (page 12). Bake 7 to 9 minutes or until sugar melts and bubbles and chips feel firm.   *Makes 6 servings*

CINNAMON-SUGAR CHIPS

    1 tablespoon margarine
1½ teaspoons water
¼ cup firmly packed brown sugar
1½ teaspoons ground cinnamon
    6 (6- to 7-inch) flour tortillas

1 Prepare chips as directed above. Add cinnamon to sugar mixture before spreading over tortillas.   *Makes 6 servings*

FIERY SWEET CHIPS

    1 tablespoon margarine
1½ teaspoons water
¼ cup firmly packed brown sugar
    6 (6- to 7-inch) flour tortillas
    Cayenne pepper

1 Prepare chips as directed above. Lightly sprinkle chips with cayenne pepper before baking.   *Makes 6 servings*

CHILE-CHEESE QUESADILLAS WITH SALSA CRUDA

❖
❖   ❖

*Substituting a combination
of low fat Monterey Jack and
ricotta cheese for regular
Monterey Jack reduces the
fat in this recipe by 60%.*

❖
❖   ❖

Nutrients per serving:

Calories	167
(21% of calories from fat)	
Total Fat	4 g
Saturated Fat	1 g
Cholesterol	7 mg
Sodium	172 mg
Carbohydrate	25 g
Dietary Fiber	3 g
Protein	10 g
Calcium	242 mg
Iron	1 mg
Vitamin A	87 RE
Vitamin C	25 mg

DIETARY EXCHANGES:
1½ Starch/Bread, ½ Lean
Meat, ½ Vegetable, ½ Fat

2 tablespoons part-skim ricotta cheese
6 (6-inch) corn tortillas
½ cup (2 ounces) shredded reduced fat Monterey Jack cheese
2 tablespoons diced mild green chilies
   Nonstick cooking spray
   Salsa Cruda (recipe follows)

1 To make 1 quesadilla, spread 2 teaspoons ricotta over tortilla. Sprinkle with heaping tablespoonful Monterey Jack cheese and 2 teaspoons diced chilies. Top with 1 tortilla. Repeat to make 2 more quesadillas.

2 Spray small nonstick skillet with cooking spray. Heat over medium-high heat. Add 1 quesadilla; cook 2 minutes or until bottom is golden. Turn quesadilla over; cook 2 minutes. Remove from heat. Cut into 4 wedges. Repeat with remaining quesadillas. Serve warm with Salsa Cruda.   *Makes 4 servings*

SALSA CRUDA

   1 cup chopped tomato
   2 tablespoons minced onion
   2 tablespoons minced fresh cilantro (optional)
   2 tablespoons lime juice
½ jalapeño pepper, seeded, minced
   1 clove garlic, minced

1 Combine tomato, onion, cilantro, lime juice, jalapeño and garlic in small bowl. Stir to combine.   *Makes 4 servings*

NACHOS

❖

These nachos combine beans, corn and cheese to create a complete protein equal to that in meat—but without the fat.

❖

Nutrients per serving:

Calories	202
(21% of calories from fat)	
Total Fat	5 g
Saturated Fat	1 g
Cholesterol	6 mg
Sodium	455 mg
Carbohydrate	29 g
Dietary Fiber	6 g
Protein	13 g
Calcium	246 mg
Iron	1 mg
Vitamin A	103 RE
Vitamin C	9 mg

DIETARY EXCHANGES:
1½ Starch/Bread, 1 Lean
Meat, 1 Vegetable, ½ Fat

8 (6-inch) corn tortillas
1 cup chopped onion
1 tablespoon chili powder
2 teaspoons dried oregano leaves, crushed
1 can (15 ounces) pinto beans *or* black beans, rinsed and drained
1¼ cups (5 ounces) shredded reduced fat Monterey Jack cheese
¾ cup frozen whole kernel corn, thawed, drained
1 jar (2 ounces) pimientos, drained
3 tablespoons ripe olive slices
2 to 3 tablespoons pickled jalapeño pepper slices, drained
　Nonstick cooking spray

1 Preheat oven to 375°F. Bake corn tortillas according to directions for Baked Tortilla Chips (page 12), baking 8 tortillas instead of 6. Arrange chips on baking sheet or in two 9-inch pie plates. Set aside.

2 Spray bottom of medium saucepan with cooking spray. Cook and stir onion over medium-high heat 8 to 10 minutes or until onion is tender and beginning to brown. Add chili powder and oregano; stir 1 minute more.

3 Remove from heat. Add beans and 2 tablespoons water; mash with fork or potato masher until blended yet chunky. Return to heat. Cover; cook beans, stirring occasionally, 6 to 8 minutes or until bubbly. Stir in additional water if beans become dry. Remove from heat. Set beans aside.

4 Sprinkle cheese evenly over chips. Spoon beans over chips.

5 Combine corn and pimientos; spoon over beans. Bake about 8 minutes or until cheese melts. Sprinkle olives and jalapeños over top. *Makes 8 servings*

GRILLED SPICED HALIBUT, PINEAPPLE AND PEPPER SKEWERS

You will get nearly half your daily requirement of vitamin C from the pineapple and peppers on just two of these tasty skewers. You will also get only one gram of fat from the halibut, which is among the fish lowest in fat and cholesterol.

❖

Nutrients per serving:

Calories	64
(15% of calories from fat)	
Total Fat	1 g
Saturated Fat	<1 g
Cholesterol	12 mg
Sodium	23 mg
Carbohydrate	6 g
Dietary Fiber	1 g
Protein	8 g
Calcium	23 mg
Iron	1 mg
Vitamin A	30 RE
Vitamin C	18 mg

DIETARY EXCHANGES:
1 Lean Meat, ½ Vegetable

2 tablespoons lemon juice or lime juice
1 teaspoon minced garlic
1 teaspoon chili powder
½ teaspoon ground cumin
¼ teaspoon ground cinnamon
⅛ teaspoon ground cloves
½ pound boneless skinless halibut steak, about 1 inch thick
½ small pineapple, peeled, halved lengthwise, cut into 24 pieces
1 large green or red bell pepper, cut into 24 squares

1 Combine lemon juice, garlic, chili powder, cumin, cinnamon and cloves in large resealable food storage bag; knead until blended.

2 Rinse fish and pat dry. Cut into 12 cubes about 1 to 1¼ inch square. Add fish to bag; press out air and seal. Turn bag gently to coat fish with marinade. Refrigerate halibut 30 minutes to 1 hour. Soak 12 (6- to 8-inch) bamboo skewers in water while fish marinates.

3 Alternately thread 2 pieces pineapple, 2 pieces pepper and 1 piece fish onto each skewer.

4 Spray cold grid with nonstick cooking spray. Adjust grid 4 to 6 inches above heat. Preheat grill to medium-high heat. Place skewers on grill, cover if possible (or tent with foil) and grill 3 to 4 minutes or until marks are established on bottom. Turn and grill skewers 3 to 4 minutes or until fish is opaque and flakes easily when tested with fork.

Makes 6 servings

GRILLED SCALLOP CEVICHE

❖

Scallops are extremely lean. One sea scallop (about one ounce) contains just half a gram of fat, yet provides about one-fifth of your daily protein.

❖

Nutrients per serving:

Calories	120
(5% of calories from fat)	
Total Fat	1 g
Saturated Fat	0 g
Cholesterol	15 mg
Sodium	164 mg
Carbohydrate	23 g
Dietary Fiber	3 g
Protein	8 g
Calcium	64 mg
Iron	1 mg
Vitamin A	40 RE
Vitamin C	80 mg

DIETARY EXCHANGES:
1 Lean Meat, 1½ Fruit

6 to 7 ounces sea scallops, 1 to 2 inches in diameter
¼ cup lime juice, divided
¼ teaspoon chili powder *or* paprika
½ large honeydew melon
1 ripe medium papaya or mango, *or* ½ large cantaloupe
¼ cup minced onion
1 to 2 fresh jalapeño *or* serrano peppers, seeded, minced
3 tablespoons minced fresh mint *or* fresh basil
1 teaspoon honey (optional)

1 Rinse scallops and pat dry. Place scallops, 2 tablespoons lime juice and chili powder in large resealable food storage bag. Press air from bag and seal. Marinate scallops in refrigerator 30 minutes to 1 hour.

2 Scoop seeds from melon. Remove fruit from rind with melon baller or cut melon into ¾-inch wedges; remove rind and cut fruit into cubes. Halve papaya, scoop out seeds, remove peel with knife; cut fruit into cubes. Place fruit into nonmetallic bowl. Stir in remaining 2 tablespoons lime juice, onion and jalapeño. Cover and refrigerate.

3 Spray cold grid with nonstick cooking spray. Adjust grid 4 to 6 inches above heat. Preheat grill to medium-high heat.

4 Drain scallops; discard marinade. Thread scallops onto 10- to 12-inch metal skewers. Grill skewers 3 minutes or until marks are established. Turn skewers over; grill 3 minutes more or until scallops are opaque.

5 Remove scallops from skewers; cut into quarters. Stir into fruit mixture. Refrigerate until thoroughly chilled, about 30 minutes or up to 24 hours. Stir in mint and honey, if desired.

Makes 6 servings

Soups & Salads

FRUIT SALAD WITH JALAPEÑO-CITRUS DRESSING

❖

On an average day, 1 out of 10 adults eats no fruit at all. Here is a striking salad that will entice everyone to indulge, packing away lots of vitamins B and C, folic acid and fiber.

❖

½ small honeydew melon
1 ripe large papaya, peeled, seeded, cubed
1 pint strawberries, stemmed, halved
1 can (8 ounces) pineapple chunks, drained
   Jalapeño-Citrus Dressing (recipe follows)

1 Scoop seeds from melon. Remove fruit from rind with melon baller or cut melon into ¾-inch wedges; remove rind and cut fruit into cubes. Place in large bowl.

2 Add papaya, strawberries, pineapple and Jalapeño-Citrus Dressing; gently toss to combine. Serve immediately or cover and refrigerate up to 3 hours. Garnish with mint leaves, if desired.

Makes 6 servings

JALAPEÑO–CITRUS DRESSING

⅓ cup orange juice
3 tablespoons lime juice
3 tablespoons minced fresh mint, basil *or* cilantro (optional)
2 jalapeño peppers, seeded, minced
1 tablespoon sugar *or* honey

1 Combine orange juice, lime juice, mint, jalapeños and sugar in small bowl; mix well.

Makes 6 servings

Nutrients per serving:	
Calories	127
(3% of calories from fat)	
Total Fat	<1 g
Saturated Fat	0 g
Cholesterol	0 mg
Sodium	153 mg
Carbohydrate	31 g
Dietary Fiber	4 g
Protein	1 g
Calcium	42 mg
Iron	1 mg
Vitamin A	39 RE
Vitamin C	115 mg

DIETARY EXCHANGES:
2 Fruit

CHILI-CRUSTED GRILLED CHICKEN CAESAR SALAD

❖

Not only is this salad low in fat, it is also full of B-vitamins and iron, as well as folic acid, a nutrient linked with the prevention of some birth defects.

❖

Nutrients per serving:

Calories	301
(28% of calories from fat)	
Total Fat	9 g
Saturated Fat	3 g
Cholesterol	64 mg
Sodium	457 mg
Carbohydrate	25 g
Dietary Fiber	5 g
Protein	31 g
Calcium	211 mg
Iron	4 mg
Vitamin A	483 RE
Vitamin C	49 mg

DIETARY EXCHANGES:
1½ Starch/Bread, 3 Lean
Meat, 1 Vegetable

1 to 2 lemons
1 tablespoon minced garlic, divided
1½ teaspoons dried oregano leaves, crushed, divided
1 teaspoon chili powder
1 pound boneless skinless chicken breasts
1 tablespoon olive oil
2 anchovy fillets, minced
1 large head romaine lettuce, cut into 1-inch strips
¼ cup grated Parmesan cheese
4 whole wheat rolls
   Parmesan Chips (page 12) (optional)

1 Grate lemon peel; measure 1 to 2 teaspoons. Juice lemon; measure ¼ cup. Combine lemon peel and 1 tablespoon juice in small bowl. Set ¼ teaspoon garlic aside. Add remaining garlic, 1 teaspoon oregano and chili powder to bowl; stir to combine. Rub chicken completely with chili mixture.

2 Combine remaining 3 tablespoons lemon juice, reserved ¼ teaspoon garlic, remaining ½ teaspoon oregano, oil and anchovy in large bowl. Add lettuce to bowl; toss to coat with dressing. Sprinkle with cheese; toss.

3 Spray cold grid with nonstick cooking spray. Adjust grid 4 to 6 inches above heat. Preheat grill to medium-high heat. Grill chicken 5 to 6 minutes or until marks are established and surface is dry. Turn chicken over; grill 3 to 4 minutes or until chicken is no longer pink in center.

4 Arrange salad on 4 large plates. Slice chicken. Fan on each salad. Serve with whole wheat rolls. Garnish with Parmesan Tortilla Chips, if desired.   *Makes 4 servings*

GAZPACHO

❖

Cool and crisp, this chilled soup of Spanish origin is a refreshing way to get lots of vegetables and fiber. Peppers and tomatoes are a great source of vitamin C—more in just a small bowl than in an orange.

❖

Nutrients per serving:

Calories	209
(23% of calories from fat)	
Total Fat	6 g
Saturated Fat	1 g
Cholesterol	0 mg
Sodium	583 mg
Carbohydrate	37 g
Dietary Fiber	6 g
Protein	7 g
Calcium	83 mg
Iron	3 mg
Vitamin A	257 RE
Vitamin C	93 mg

DIETARY EXCHANGES:
1½ Starch/Bread,
2 Vegetable, 1 Fat

2 large cucumbers, peeled, seeded, divided
12 roma tomatoes, divided
 1 cup chopped yellow or green bell pepper, divided
⅓ cup green onions, sliced, divided
 1 cup ⅓-less-salt chicken broth
½ cup low sodium vegetable juice cocktail
½ teaspoon dried thyme leaves, crushed
 3 tablespoons red wine vinegar
¼ to ½ teaspoon hot pepper sauce
 1 can (2¼ ounces) sliced ripe olives
 3 tablespoons crumbled feta cheese (optional)
 2 teaspoons drained capers (optional)
 6 whole wheat rolls

1 Chop 1 cucumber and 9 tomatoes. Combine chopped cucumber, tomatoes, ½ cup pepper, 2 tablespoons green onions, broth, vegetable juice and thyme in food processor or blender; process until puréed (if necessary do in 2 batches). Pour into fine wire strainer set over large bowl. Rub back of spoon over bottom of strainer until all that remains are vegetable skins and seeds; discard. Skim foam from juice. Add vinegar and hot pepper sauce.

2 Chop remaining cucumber and 3 tomatoes. Combine with remaining ½ cup pepper and green onions. Add vegetables to puréed mixture. Cover and chill thoroughly 2 hours or up to 24 hours. Top with olives. Garnish with cheese and capers, if desired. Serve with whole wheat rolls.

Makes 6 servings

LAYERED MEXICAN SALAD

❖

No sense denying yourself old favorites simply because they do not fall into the guidelines of a low fat diet. Nonfat mayonnaise and reduced fat cheese replace their regular counterparts in this Mexican version of the popular layered salad. Lots of lemon, olives, garlic and Salsa Cruda supply plenty of flavor.

❖

⅔ cup dried black turtle beans *or* 1 can (15 ounces) black turtle beans, rinsed, drained
1 small head romaine lettuce, washed, cored
  Salsa Cruda (page 14)
1 cup frozen whole kernel corn, thawed, drained
1 can (2¼ ounces) sliced ripe olives, drained
1 large cucumber, peeled
1 large lemon
¾ cup nonfat mayonnaise
3 tablespoons plain nonfat yogurt
2 to 3 cloves garlic, minced
½ cup (2 ounces) shredded low fat Cheddar cheese
1 green onion, thinly sliced

1 Rinse and sort beans. Place in medium saucepan with 2 cups water. Bring to a boil over high heat. Reduce heat to medium-low; simmer 5 minutes. Remove from heat; cover and let stand 1 to 2 hours. Drain. Return beans to pan with 2 cups fresh water. Bring to a boil. Reduce heat to medium-low; cover and simmer 1 to 2 hours or until tender. Drain and rinse.

2 Layer romaine leaves and slice crosswise into ½-inch strips. Place half of lettuce in large serving bowl. Layer Salsa Cruda, beans and corn over lettuce.

3 Halve cucumber lengthwise; scoop out and discard seeds. Slice thinly. Place cucumber over corn, sprinkle with olives and top with remaining lettuce.

4 Grate lemon peel; combine with mayonnaise, yogurt and garlic. Juice lemon; stir 3 to 4 tablespoons juice into dressing. Spread dressing evenly over top of salad. Sprinkle with cheese and green onion. Cover salad and refrigerate 2 hours or up to 1 day.

Makes 12 servings

Nutrients per serving:

Calories	117
(22% of calories from fat)	
Total Fat	3 g
Saturated Fat	1 g
Cholesterol	3 mg
Sodium	349 mg
Carbohydrate	19 g
Dietary Fiber	3 g
Protein	6 g
Calcium	77 mg
Iron	2 mg
Vitamin A	121 RE
Vitamin C	18 mg

DIETARY EXCHANGES:
1 Starch/Bread,
1 Vegetable, 1 Fat

SPINACH SALAD WITH ORANGE-CHILI GLAZED SHRIMP

❖

This is about as close to perfectly balanced as one dish can get. In addition to being a rich source of vitamins A and C, fiber, calcium and iron, this salad is also high in protein, vitamin B, folic acid, potassium and other trace minerals.

❖

Nutrients per serving:

Calories	177
(29% of calories from fat)	
Total Fat	6 g
Saturated Fat	3 g
Cholesterol	100 mg
Sodium	311 mg
Carbohydrate	19 g
Dietary Fiber	3 g
Protein	14 g
Calcium	165 mg
Iron	3 mg
Vitamin A	671 RE
Vitamin C	57 mg

DIETARY EXCHANGES:
1½ Lean Meat, 1 Fruit,
1 Vegetable

2 teaspoons sesame seeds
¼ cup orange juice
1 tablespoon cider vinegar
1 clove garlic, minced
1 teaspoon grated orange peel
1 teaspoon olive oil
½ teaspoon honey
⅛ teaspoon crushed red pepper
1 ripe large mango *or* ripe medium papaya
12 cups washed and torn fresh spinach leaves
½ cup crumbled feta cheese
Orange-Chili Glazed Shrimp (recipe follows)

1 Heat small nonstick skillet over medium heat. Add sesame seeds and cook, stirring often, about 4 minutes or until golden. Pour into small bowl. Add orange juice, vinegar, garlic, orange peel, oil, honey and red pepper; stir to combine. Set aside.

2 Peel mango. Cut fruit away from pit; cut into cubes or slices. Discard tough stems from spinach leaves. Place leaves into large bowl and toss with dressing. Top with mango, cheese and shrimp.

Makes 4 servings

ORANGE–CHILI GLAZED SHRIMP

½ cup orange juice
4 cloves garlic, minced
1 teaspoon chili powder
8 ounces raw large shrimp, peeled, deveined

1 Combine juice, garlic and chili powder in large nonstick skillet. Bring to a boil over high heat. Boil 3 minutes or until mixture just coats bottom of pan. Reduce heat to medium. Add shrimp; cook and stir 2 minutes or until shrimp are opaque and juice mixture coats shrimp. (Add orange juice or water to keep shrimp moist, if necessary.)

Makes 4 servings

JICAMA SLAW

❖

Studies indicate that people who eat lots of foods belonging to the Brassica family, such as cabbage, have a reduced risk of various cancers, thanks to antioxidants such as vitamins A and C, and fiber.

❖

Nutrients per serving:

Calories	108
(30% of calories from fat)	
Total Fat	4 g
Saturated Fat	<1 g
Cholesterol	4 mg
Sodium	94 mg
Carbohydrate	18 g
Dietary Fiber	3 g
Protein	2 g
Calcium	54 mg
Iron	1 mg
Vitamin A	49 RE
Vitamin C	73 mg

DIETARY EXCHANGES:
1 Fruit, 1 Vegetable, ½ Fat

2 to 3 large oranges
½ cup minced red onion
½ cup lightly packed fresh cilantro, coarsely chopped *plus* additional cilantro for garnish
⅓ cup reduced calorie mayonnaise
2 tablespoons frozen orange juice concentrate, thawed
1 tablespoon sugar
1 jalapeño *or* serrano pepper, seeded, minced
4 cups shredded jicama*
3 cups shredded green cabbage

1 Grate orange peel with grater or zester; measure 1 tablespoon. Place in large bowl; set aside. Cut away remaining white pith from oranges, working over bowl to collect juices. Cut between membranes to separate orange segments; set segments aside. Squeeze membranes with hand to remove more juice.

2 Add onion, cilantro, mayonnaise, orange juice concentrate, sugar and jalapeño.

3 Add jicama and cabbage; stir to combine. Reserve several orange segments for garnish; cut remaining segments in half and stir into slaw. Transfer slaw to serving bowl and garnish with orange curls and cilantro. *Makes 6 servings*

*Peel jicama with sharp knife, removing brown outer skin and thin coarse layer of flesh underneath. Shred jicama in food processor.

POZOLE

❖

No one knows exactly why, but studies have proven chicken soup has a soothing effect on cold symptoms.

❖

Nutrients per serving:

Calories	241
(27% of calories from fat)	
Total Fat	7 g
Saturated Fat	1 g
Cholesterol	39 mg
Sodium	584 mg
Carbohydrate	26 g
Dietary Fiber	5 g
Protein	19 g
Calcium	88 mg
Iron	3 mg
Vitamin A	52 RE
Vitamin C	49 mg

DIETARY EXCHANGES:
1 Starch/Bread, 1½ Lean
Meat, 2 Vegetable, 1 Fat

3 (6-inch) corn tortillas
  Nonstick cooking spray
1 large onion, chopped
1 tablespoon minced garlic
1 tablespoon dried oregano leaves, crushed
1½ teaspoons ground cumin
2 cans (14½ ounces each) ⅓-less-salt chicken broth *plus* water to make 5 cups
1 pound boneless skinless chicken breasts
2 cans (15 ounces each) yellow hominy, drained
1 red or green bell pepper, chopped
1 can (4 ounces) diced mild green chilies
1 can (2¼ ounces) sliced ripe olives, drained
½ cup lightly packed fresh cilantro, coarsely chopped

1 Preheat oven to 450°F.

2 Cut tortillas into ¼-inch-wide strips. Place strips in single layer on baking sheet. Bake 3 to 4 minutes or until crisp. Do not let strips brown. Remove strips to plate to cool while preparing soup.

3 Coat bottom of large saucepan with cooking spray. Heat over medium heat until hot. Add onion, garlic, oregano and cumin; stir to combine. Cover pan and cook, stirring occasionally, about 6 minutes or until onion is golden. Add broth and water; cover and bring to a boil over high heat. Add chicken. Cover; reduce heat to low and simmer 8 minutes or until chicken is no longer pink in center. Remove chicken from broth and let cool slightly; cut into ½-inch cubes.

4 Meanwhile, add hominy, pepper, chilies and olives to broth. Cover and bring to a boil over medium-high heat. Reduce heat to medium-low; simmer 4 minutes or until pepper is crisp-tender. Return chicken to saucepan. Stir in cilantro. Top with toasted tortilla strips.

Makes 6 servings

ROASTED PEPPER, CORN AND BEAN SALAD

❖

Sweet and hot peppers have gained immense popularity with nutritionists worldwide. One red bell pepper has 16 times the beta carotene and nearly twice the vitamin C of one orange.

❖

1 large red bell pepper
2 cans (15 ounces each) black turtle beans, garbanzo beans (chick peas), pinto *or* kidney beans
1 cup frozen whole kernel corn, thawed, drained
1 can (4 ounces) diced mild green chilies
2 green onions, thinly sliced
Cumin Dressing (recipe follows)

1 Place pepper on pan under preheated broiler 2 inches from heat. Broil 15 to 18 minutes, turning pepper as each side becomes charred. Invert bowl over pepper (or place in resealable food storage bag) until cool. Rub charred skin from pepper (all skin need not come off). Working over large bowl, cut stem from pepper; let juice run into bowl. Quarter pepper lengthwise; discard seeds. Slice crosswise; add to bowl.

2 Rinse and drain beans well; add to pepper. Add corn, chilies, green onions and Cumin Dressing; stir. Cover and refrigerate 1 hour or up to 24 hours. Serve on lettuce-lined plate garnished with green onion fans, if desired.   *Makes 8 servings*

CUMIN DRESSING

2 tablespoons white wine vinegar or cider vinegar
2 tablespoons lemon juice
1 teaspoon grated lemon peel
1 clove garlic, minced
½ teaspoon ground cumin

1 Combine all ingredients in small bowl; mix well.   *Makes 8 servings*

Nutrients per serving:	
Calories	128
(10% of calories from fat)	
Total Fat	2 g
Saturated Fat	<1 g
Cholesterol	0 mg
Sodium	380 mg
Carbohydrate	26 g
Dietary Fiber	7 g
Protein	8 g
Calcium	30 mg
Iron	2 mg
Vitamin A	35 RE
Vitamin C	54 mg

DIETARY EXCHANGES:
1 Starch/Bread, ½ Lean Meat, 1 Vegetable

TORTILLA DISHES

SEAFOOD TACOS WITH FRUIT SALSA

Naturally low in fat, seafood adds a delicious touch to these tacos.

2 tablespoons lemon juice
1 teaspoon chili powder
1 teaspoon ground allspice
1 teaspoon olive oil
1 teaspoon minced garlic
1 to 2 teaspoons grated lemon peel
½ teaspoon ground cloves
1 pound halibut *or* snapper fillets
3 cups shredded romaine lettuce
1 small red onion, halved, thinly sliced
12 (6-inch) corn tortillas *or* 6 (7- to 8-inch) flour tortillas
Fruit Salsa (page 40)

1 Combine lemon juice, chili powder, allspice, oil, garlic, lemon peel and cloves in small bowl. Rub fish with spice mixture; cover and refrigerate while grill heats, or refrigerate up to several hours. (Fish may be cut into smaller pieces for easier handling.)

2 Spray cold grid with nonstick cooking spray. Adjust grid 4 to 6 inches above heat. Preheat grill to medium-high heat. Grill, covered, 3 minutes or until fish is lightly seared on bottom. Carefully turn fish over; grill 2 minutes or until fish is opaque in center and flakes easily when tested with fork. Remove from heat and cut into 12 pieces, removing bones if necessary. Cover to keep warm.

3 Place tortillas on grill in single layer and cook 5 to 10 seconds; turn over and cook another 5 to 10 seconds or until hot and pliable. Stack; cover to keep warm.

4 Top each tortilla with ¼ cup lettuce and red onion. Add 1 piece of fish and about 2 tablespoons Fruit Salsa.

Makes 6 servings

Nutrients per serving:

includes 2 tablespoons Fruit Salsa

Calories	294
(14% of calories from fat)	
Total Fat	5 g
Saturated Fat	1 g
Cholesterol	24 mg
Sodium	296 mg
Carbohydrate	43 g
Dietary Fiber	6 g
Protein	21 g
Calcium	162 mg
Iron	3 mg
Vitamin A	171 RE
Vitamin C	68 mg

DIETARY EXCHANGES:
1½ Starch/Bread, 2 Lean Meat, 1 Fruit, ½ Vegetable

(continued on page 40)

Seafood Tacos with Fruit Salsa, continued

FRUIT SALSA

    1 small ripe papaya, peeled, seeded, diced
    1 firm small banana, diced
    2 green onions, minced
    3 tablespoons chopped fresh cilantro *or* fresh mint
    3 tablespoons lime juice
    2 jalapeño peppers, seeded, minced

1 Combine all ingredients in small bowl. Serve at room temperature.

Makes 12 servings

❖

Health Note

Halibut is a white, firm and mild-flavored fish which is low in fat and also lower in cholesterol and sodium than many other kinds of fish.

❖

CHICKEN, SPINACH & RAISIN ENCHILADAS

With just one-fourth the calories from fat, more than 100% of daily vitamins A and C, half the calcium and plenty of B-complex vitamins and iron, this is one enchilada you can eat without guilt (pictured on page 43).

Nutrients per serving:

includes Roasted Tomato Enchilada Sauce

Calories	401
(23% of calories from fat)	
Total Fat	11 g
Saturated Fat	4 g
Cholesterol	43 mg
Sodium	283 mg
Carbohydrate	51 g
Dietary Fiber	8 g
Protein	30 g
Calcium	561 mg
Iron	4 mg
Vitamin A	624 RE
Vitamin C	49 mg

DIETARY EXCHANGES:
2 Starch/Bread, 3 Lean Meat, 1/2 Fruit, 2 Vegetable, 1/2 Fat

2 boneless skinless chicken breasts (5 ounces each)
1 package (10 ounces) frozen chopped spinach, thawed, well drained
1½ cups (6 ounces) shredded reduced fat Monterey Jack cheese, divided
¾ cup part-skim ricotta cheese
½ cup raisins *or* currants
¼ teaspoon ground cloves
12 (6-inch) corn tortillas
   Roasted Tomato Enchilada Sauce (page 42)

1 Preheat oven to 350°F.

2 Bring 4 cups water to a boil over high heat in large saucepan. Add chicken. Cover; remove from heat. Let stand 15 minutes or until chicken is no longer pink in center. Drain; cool slightly and tear into small pieces. Place spinach in large bowl with 1 cup Monterey Jack cheese, ricotta cheese, raisins and cloves; stir to combine. Stir in chicken.

3 Heat large nonstick skillet over medium-high heat. Place 1 inch water in medium bowl. Dip 1 tortilla in water; shake off excess. Place in hot skillet. Cook 10 to 15 seconds on each side or until tortilla is hot and pliable. Repeat with remaining tortillas.

4 Spray 13×9-inch baking dish with nonstick cooking spray. Place 1 cup Roasted Tomato Enchilada Sauce in large bowl. Dip tortillas 1 at a time into sauce; shake off excess. Spread ⅓ cup chicken mixture in center of each tortilla; fold sides over to enclose and place seam side down in pan. Spread remaining Enchilada Sauce over enchiladas. Cover pan tightly with foil. Recipe can be refrigerated up to 24 hours at this point.

5 Bake 30 to 40 minutes or until heated through. Sprinkle with remaining ½ cup Monterey Jack cheese. Bake 3 minutes or until cheese melts. *Makes 6 servings*

(continued on page 42)

Chicken, Spinach & Raisin Enchiladas, continued

ROASTED TOMATO ENCHILADA SAUCE

- 2 pounds small tomatoes
- 1 red bell pepper
- 4 cloves garlic, unpeeled
- 2 teaspoons olive oil
- 1 small onion, chopped
- 1 tablespoon chili powder
- ½ teaspoon ground cinnamon
- ¼ teaspoon ground cloves

1 Place tomatoes, pepper and garlic in 13×9-inch baking dish. Broil 2 inches from heat 8 to 9 minutes or until vegetables are browned in spots. Turn vegetables; repeat 2 more times until vegetables are browned on all sides.

2 Place tomatoes in food processor or blender, discarding any liquid remaining in pan. Peel skin from pepper and remove stem and seeds. Add pepper to tomatoes. Slice open garlic cloves and press into tomato mixture; process until smooth. Set aside.

3 Meanwhile, heat oil over medium-high heat in large saucepan. Add onion; cook and stir 4 minutes or until tender. Add chili powder, cinnamon and cloves. Continue cooking 1 minute. Reduce heat to medium-low. Pour tomato mixture into pan and simmer, uncovered, 10 minutes or until heated through. Serve immediately.

Makes 6 servings

LEMON CHEESE QUESADILLAS WITH MANGO SAUCE

With lots of vitamins, calcium and protein, this light breakfast or brunch is a refreshing change from the usual morning fare.

❖

Nutrients per serving:

Calories	283
(20% of calories from fat)	
Total Fat	6 g
Saturated Fat	3 g
Cholesterol	17 mg
Sodium	246 mg
Carbohydrate	48 g
Dietary Fiber	4 g
Protein	11 g
Calcium	248 mg
Iron	2 mg
Vitamin A	290 RE
Vitamin C	50 mg

DIETARY EXCHANGES:
1 Starch/Bread, 2 Fruit,
1/2 Fat

4 (7-inch) flour tortillas
1 cup part-skim ricotta cheese
⅓ cup nonfat vanilla yogurt
¼ cup lemon juice, divided
1½ tablespoons sugar
2 teaspoons grated lemon peel
1 teaspoon vanilla
1 ripe large mango
2 tablespoons lightly packed fresh mint, fresh cilantro *or* fresh basil,
　　plus 4 sprigs for garnish
½ jalapeño pepper, seeded, minced (optional)
1 firm ripe banana, sliced into ¼-inch-thick rounds
½ pint fresh strawberries, quartered

1 Preheat oven to 375°F.

2 Place tortillas on center oven rack. Bake 6 to 7 minutes or until golden. Place on plate.

3 Combine ricotta, yogurt, 1 tablespoon lemon juice, sugar, lemon peel and vanilla in small bowl. Spread about ⅓ cup over each tortilla.

4 Peel mango. Cut fruit away from pit; chop fruit into ½-inch cubes. Place half of mango in food processor or blender. Add 2 tablespoons lemon juice, mint and jalapeño; process until puréed.

5 Place remaining mango cubes in small bowl with banana, strawberries and remaining 1 tablespoon lemon juice; toss gently to combine. Spoon ½ cup fruit on each tortilla. Drizzle with about 1 tablespoon sauce. Garnish with mint sprigs.

Makes 4 servings

TOSTADAS

Mexico's version of the chef salad, tostadas offer as much room for variety as for flavor. A good source of vitamins A and C, iron, calcium and fiber, this light, meatless meal also provides over one-third your daily requirement of high quality protein.

½ small avocado (optional)
3 tablespoons nonfat plain yogurt (optional)
1 teaspoon lemon juice (optional)
4 (7-inch) flour tortillas
1 small onion, chopped
1 tablespoon chili powder
2 teaspoons dried oregano leaves, crushed
1 can (15 ounces) pinto beans, drained, rinsed
4 cups shredded romaine lettuce
1 cup (4 ounces) shredded reduced fat Cheddar cheese
   Salsa Cruda (page 14)
3 tablespoons sliced ripe olives

1 Preheat oven to 375°F. If desired, combine avocado, yogurt and lemon juice in food processor or blender; process until smooth. Set aside.

2 Place tortillas in single layer on center rack of oven. Bake 5 minutes or until crisp and golden, turning halfway through baking. Set aside.

3 Spray large skillet with nonstick cooking spray and heat over medium heat. Add onion; cook and stir 10 minutes or until onion begins to brown. Add chili powder and oregano; cook and stir 1 minute. Remove from heat; stir in beans and ¼ cup water. Mash beans with fork until smooth; if necessary, add more water, 1 tablespoon at a time. Return to heat. Cover and cook, stirring occasionally, 6 minutes or until heated through.

4 Place each tortilla on plate. Spread ⅓ cup beans over each tortilla. Top beans with 1 cup lettuce, ¼ cup cheese, ¼ cup Salsa Cruda and about 2 teaspoons olives. Garnish with avocado mixture in cherry tomato cup, if desired.   *Makes 4 servings*

Nutrients per serving:

Calories	380
(20% of calories from fat)	
Total Fat	9 g
Saturated Fat	2 g
Cholesterol	10 mg
Sodium	509 mg
Carbohydrate	55 g
Dietary Fiber	11 g
Protein	23 g
Calcium	451 mg
Iron	6 mg
Vitamin A	317 RE
Vitamin C	32 mg

DIETARY EXCHANGES:
3 Starch/Bread, 1½ Lean
Meat, 2 Vegetable, ½ Fat

FAJITAS

❖

There are as many versions of fajitas as there are restaurants preparing them. A low fat, generally chewy piece of meat is made tender by quick cooking, then slicing thinly across the prominent lengthwise grain. Lots of roasted bell peppers, rich in vitamin C, are standard.

❖

Nutrients per serving:

Calories	304
(28% of calories from fat)	
Total Fat	9 g
Saturated Fat	4 g
Cholesterol	44 mg
Sodium	198 mg
Carbohydrate	25 g
Dietary Fiber	3 g
Protein	30 g
Calcium	78 mg
Iron	4 mg
Vitamin A	129 RE
Vitamin C	63 mg

DIETARY EXCHANGES:
1 Starch/Bread, 3 Lean
Meat, 2 Vegetable, ½ Fat

Fajita Marinande (page 50)
1 pound flank steak
4 bell peppers, any color, halved
1 large bunch green onions
6 (10-inch) flour tortillas *or* 12 (7-inch) flour tortillas
Salsa Cruda (page 14)
1 cup coarsely chopped fresh cilantro
1 ripe avocado, peeled, pitted, thinly sliced (optional)
6 tablespoons low fat sour cream (optional)

1 Combine Fajita Marinade and flank steak in resealable plastic food storage bag. Press air from bag and seal. Refrigerate 30 minutes or up to 24 hours.

2 Place tortillas in stacks of 3. Wrap each stack in aluminum foil; set aside.

3 Drain marinade from meat into small saucepan. Bring to a boil over high heat. Remove from heat.

4 Spray cold grid with nonstick cooking spray. Adjust grid 4 to 6 inches above heat. Preheat grill to medium-high heat. Place meat in center of grill. Place peppers, skin side down, around meat; cover. Grill peppers 6 minutes or until skin is spotted with brown. Turn over and continue grilling 6 to 8 minutes or until tender. Move to sides of grill to keep warm while meat finishes grilling. Grill meat, basting frequently with marinade, 8 minutes or until browned on bottom. Turn over; grill 8 to 10 minutes or until slightly pink in center. During the last 4 minutes of grilling, brush onions with remaining marinade and place on grill; grill 1 to 2 minutes or until browned in spots. Turn over; grill 1 to 2 minutes or until tender.

5 Place packets of tortillas on grill; heat about 5 minutes. Slice peppers and onions into thin 2-inch-long pieces. Thinly slice meat across the grain.

6 Place tortilla on plate. Place meat, peppers, onions, Salsa Cruda and cilantro in center of each tortilla. Fold sides completely over filling to enclose. Serve with avocado and sour cream, if desired.

Makes 6 servings

(continued on page 50)

Fajitas, continued

FAJITA MARINADE

½ cup lime juice *or* ¼ cup lime juice and ¼ cup tequilla or beer
1 tablespoon dried oregano leaves, crushed
1 tablespoon minced garlic
2 teaspoons ground cumin
2 teaspoons black pepper

1 Combine lime juice, oregano, garlic, cumin and black pepper in 1-cup glass measure. Stir to combine.

❖

Health Note

Bell peppers are naturally delicious and grilling them at medium-high heat gives them a wonderful new flavor complexity without adding any fat.

❖

CRAB AND CORN ENCHILADA CASSEROLE

❖

This casserole shares an important trait with other one-dish meals; it provides substantial amounts of a wide array of key nutrients, including vitamins A, C and B-complex, plus the minerals iron and calcium. What an easy way to get a balanced meal. This casserole is pictured on page 53.

❖

Nutrients per serving:

includes Spicy Tomato Sauce

Calories	366
(20% of calories from fat)	
Total Fat	9 g
Saturated Fat	2 g
Cholesterol	46 mg
Sodium	343 mg
Carbohydrate	51 g
Dietary Fiber	7 g
Protein	27 g
Calcium	467 mg
Iron	4 mg
Vitamin A	292 RE
Vitamin C	71 mg

DIETARY EXCHANGES:
2$\frac{1}{2}$ Starch/Bread, 2$\frac{1}{2}$ Lean Meat, 2 Vegetable

Spicy Tomato Sauce (page 52), divided
10 to 12 ounces fresh crabmeat *or* flaked or chopped surimi crab
1 package (10 ounces) frozen whole kernel corn, thawed, drained
1$\frac{1}{2}$ cups (6 ounces) shredded reduced fat Monterey Jack cheese, divided
1 can (4 ounces) diced mild green chilies
12 (6-inch) corn tortillas
1 lime, cut into 6 wedges
Low fat sour cream (optional)

1 Preheat oven to 350°F.

2 Combine 2 cups Spicy Tomato Sauce, crab, corn, 1 cup cheese and chilies in medium bowl.

3 Cut each tortilla into 4 wedges. Place one-third of tortilla wedges in bottom of shallow 3- to 4-quart casserole, overlapping to make solid layer. Spread half of crab mixture on top. Repeat with another layer tortilla wedges, remaining crab mixture and remaining tortillas. Spread remaining 1 cup Spicy Tomato Sauce over top; cover.

4 Bake 30 to 40 minutes or until heated through. Sprinkle with remaining $\frac{1}{2}$ cup cheese and bake uncovered 5 minutes or until cheese melts. Squeeze lime over individual servings. Serve with low fat sour cream, if desired.   *Makes 6 servings*

(continued on page 52)

Crab and Corn Enchilada Casserole, continued

SPICY TOMATO SAUCE

    2 cans (15 ounces each) no-salt-added stewed tomatoes, undrained *or* 6 medium tomatoes

    2 teaspoons olive oil

    1 medium onion, chopped

    1 tablespoon minced garlic

    2 tablespoons chili powder

    2 teaspoons ground cumin

    2 teaspoons dried oregano leaves, crushed

    1 teaspoon ground cinnamon

    $\frac{1}{4}$ teaspoon crushed red pepper

    $\frac{1}{4}$ teaspoon ground cloves

1 Combine tomatoes with liquid in food processor or blender; process until finely chopped. Set aside.

2 Heat oil over medium-high heat in large saucepan or Dutch oven. Add onion and garlic. Cook and stir 5 minutes or until onion is tender. Add chili powder, cumin, oregano, cinnamon, red pepper and cloves. Cook and stir 1 minute.

3 Add tomatoes; reduce heat to medium-low. Simmer, uncovered, 20 minutes or until sauce is reduced to 3 to $3\frac{1}{4}$ cups.   *Makes about 3 cups*

TACOS WITH CARNITAS

❖

Carnitas are the standard filling in street tacos and tamales. Normally a fatty chuck of pork is boiled, baked and shredded to yield these "little meats." Use a lean pork roast, then mix the shredded meat back into reduced cooking broth to make a flavorful, moist replica with a minimum of fat.

❖

Nutrients per serving:

Calories	292
(24% of calories from fat)	
Total Fat	8 g
Saturated Fat	2 g
Cholesterol	55 mg
Sodium	163 mg
Carbohydrate	28 g
Dietary Fiber	2 g
Protein	28 g
Calcium	130 mg
Iron	3 mg
Vitamin A	153 RE
Vitamin C	32 mg

DIETARY EXCHANGES:
1½ Starch/Bread, 3 Lean Meat, 1 Vegetable

2 pounds pork leg, shoulder *or* butt roast, fat trimmed
1 medium onion, peeled, quartered
2 tablespoons chili powder
1 tablespoon dried oregano leaves, crushed
3 bay leaves
1 teaspoon ground cumin
16 (6-inch) corn tortillas
4 cups shredded romaine lettuce
1 cup crumbled feta cheese (optional)
1 can (4 ounces) diced mild green chilies
 Salsa Cruda (page 14)

1 Preheat oven to 450°F. Place pork, onion, chili powder, oregano, bay leaves and cumin in large saucepan or Dutch oven. Add enough water to cover pork. Cover and bring to a boil; reduce heat to medium-low. Simmer 3 hours or until meat pulls apart easily when tested with fork.

2 Transfer meat to baking pan. Bake 20 minutes or until surface is browned and crisp. Meanwhile, skim fat from cooking liquid. Boil on high heat 20 minutes or until mixture is reduced to about 1 cup. Remove and discard bay leaves.

3 Shred meat by pulling apart with 2 forks. Add meat to reduced cooking liquid; stir to coat completely. Cover; simmer 10 minutes or until meat absorbs most of liquid.

4 Heat large nonstick skillet over medium-high heat. Place 2 inches water in medium bowl. Dip 1 tortilla in water; shake off excess. Place in hot skillet. Cook 30 seconds on each side or until tortilla is hot and pliable but just starting to firm slightly. Transfer to plate and cover to keep warm. Repeat with remaining tortillas.

5 To assemble tacos, top each tortilla with ¼ cup lettuce, ¼ cup meat, 1 tablespoon cheese, if desired, 1 teaspoon chilies and 1 tablespoon Salsa Cruda.

Makes 8 servings

BEAN AND VEGETABLE BURRITOS

❖

The combination of amino acids from beans, corn, tortillas and cheese provides a high quality complete protein we often depend on meat to provide.

❖

Nutrients per serving:

Calories	428
(17% of calories from fat)	
Total Fat	9 g
Saturated Fat	2 g
Cholesterol	7 mg
Sodium	617 mg
Carbohydrate	75 g
Dietary Fiber	9 g
Protein	22 g
Calcium	320 mg
Iron	3 mg
Vitamin A	147 RE
Vitamin C	35 mg

DIETARY EXCHANGES:
4 Starch/Bread, 1 Lean
Meat, 2 Vegetable, 1 Fat

1 tablespoon olive oil
1 medium onion, thinly sliced
1 jalapeño pepper, seeded, minced
1 tablespoon chili powder
3 cloves garlic, minced
2 teaspoons dried oregano leaves, crushed
1 teaspoon ground cumin
1 large sweet potato, baked, cooled, peeled, diced *or* 1 can (16 ounces) yams in syrup, drained, rinsed, diced
1 can black beans *or* pinto beans, drained, rinsed
1 cup frozen whole kernel corn, thawed, drained
1 green bell pepper, chopped
2 tablespoons lime juice
¾ cup (3 ounces) shredded reduced fat Monterey Jack cheese
4 (10-inch) flour tortillas
Low fat sour cream (optional)

1 Preheat oven to 350°F.

2 Heat oil over medium-high heat in large saucepan or Dutch oven. Add onion and cook, stirring often, 10 minutes or until golden. Add jalapeño, chili powder, garlic, oregano and cumin; stir 1 minute more. Add 1 tablespoon water and stir; remove from heat. Stir in sweet potato, beans, corn, pepper and lime juice.

3 Spoon 2 tablespoons cheese in center of each tortilla. Top with 1 cup filling. Fold all 4 sides around filling to enclose. Place burritos seam side down on baking sheet. Cover with foil and bake 30 minutes or until heated through. Serve with sour cream, if desired.

Makes 4 servings

CHICKEN & CHILE CHIMICHANGAS

❖

Get that crisp texture the low fat way by brushing chimichangas lightly with water, then baking until tortillas are crisp and golden.

❖

Nutrients per serving:

Calories	248
(29% of calories from fat)	
Total Fat	8 g
Saturated Fat	3 g
Cholesterol	43 mg
Sodium	578 mg
Carbohydrate	23 g
Dietary Fiber	<1 g
Protein	20 g
Calcium	277 mg
Iron	2 mg
Vitamin A	159 RE
Vitamin C	17 mg

DIETARY EXCHANGES:
1¹/₂ Starch/Bread, 2 Lean Meat, ¹/₂ Vegetable, ¹/₂ Fat

2 boneless skinless chicken breast halves (5 ounces each)
¹/₂ teaspoon ground cumin
1 cup (4 ounces) shredded reduced fat Monterey Jack cheese
1 can (4 ounces) diced mild green chilies
6 (7-inch) flour tortillas
  Green Onion-Cilantro Sauce (recipe follows)

1 Preheat oven to 400°F. Bring 4 cups water to a boil in large saucepan over high heat. Add chicken, cover and remove from heat. Let stand 15 minutes or until chicken is no longer pink in center. Drain; let cool slightly. Tear into small pieces. Place in medium bowl and sprinkle with cumin. Add cheese and chilies; stir to combine.

2 Spoon about ¹/₂ cup chicken mixture down center of each tortilla. Fold bottom of tortilla up over filling, then fold sides over filling. Brush each chimichanga lightly with water, coating all around. Place on baking sheet, about 1 inch apart. Bake 12 to 15 minutes or until tortillas are crisp and just barely golden. Serve with shredded romaine lettuce, tomato slices and Green Onion-Cilantro Sauce.   *Makes 6 servings*

GREEN ONION–CILANTRO SAUCE

¹/₄ cup plain nonfat yogurt
¹/₄ cup low fat sour cream
¹/₃ cup chopped green onions
¹/₃ cup lightly packed fresh cilantro

1 Combine all ingredients in food processor or blender; process until smooth.

Makes 6 servings

TURKEY & ZUCCHINI ENCHILADAS WITH TOMATILLO-GREEN CHILE SAUCE

How many times have you been warned to stay clear of the high fat leg and thigh meat of poultry? Fat content is relative. Combined with low fat cheese, lots of fresh zucchini and corn tortillas, this succulent dark turkey meat contributes to a more flavorful, but still low fat, enchilada dinner.

1¼ pound turkey leg
1 tablespoon olive oil
1 small onion, thinly sliced
1 tablespoon minced garlic
1 pound zucchini, quartered lengthwise, sliced thinly crosswise
1½ teaspoons ground cumin
½ teaspoon dried oregano leaves, crushed
¾ cup (3 ounces) shredded reduced fat Monterey Jack cheese
12 (6-inch) corn tortillas
   Tomatillo-Green Chile Sauce (page 62)
½ cup crumbled feta cheese
6 sprigs fresh cilantro for garnish

1 Place turkey in large saucepan; cover with water. Bring to a boil over high heat. Reduce heat to medium-low. Cover and simmer 1½ to 2 hours or until meat pulls apart easily when tested with fork. Drain; discard skin and bone. Cut meat into small pieces. Place in medium bowl; set aside.

2 Preheat oven to 350°F.

3 Heat oil over medium-high heat in large skillet. Add onion; cook and stir 3 to 4 minutes or until tender. Reduce heat to medium. Add garlic; cook and stir 3 to 4 minutes or until onion is golden. Add zucchini, 2 tablespoons water, cumin and oregano. Cover; cook and stir over medium heat 10 minutes or until zucchini is tender. Add to turkey. Stir in Monterey Jack cheese.

4 Heat large nonstick skillet over medium-high heat. Place 1 inch water in medium bowl. Dip 1 tortilla in water; shake off excess. Place in hot skillet. Cook 10 to 15 seconds on each side or until tortilla is hot and pliable. Repeat with remaining tortillas.

5 Spray bottom of 13×9-inch baking pan with nonstick cooking spray. Spoon ¼ cup filling in center of each tortilla; fold sides over to enclose. Place seam side down in pan. Brush tops with ½ cup Tomatillo-Green Chile Sauce. Cover; bake 30 to 40 minutes or until heated through. Top enchiladas with remaining Tomatillo-Green Chile Sauce and feta cheese. Garnish with cilantro.

Makes 6 servings

Nutrients per serving:

Calories	377
(28% of calories from fat)	
Total Fat	12 g
Saturated Fat	3 g
Cholesterol	48 mg
Sodium	284 mg
Carbohydrate	41 g
Dietary Fiber	5 g
Protein	29 g
Calcium	320 mg
Iron	4 mg
Vitamin A	76 RE
Vitamin C	34 mg

DIETARY EXCHANGES:
2 Starch/Bread, 2½ Lean Meat, 2 Vegetable, 1 Fat

(continued on page 62)

Turkey & Zucchini Enchiladas with Tomatillo-Green Chile Sauce, continued

TOMATILLO–GREEN CHILE SAUCE

¾ pound fresh tomatillos *or*
     2 cans (18 ounces each) whole tomatillos, drained
1 can (4 ounces) diced mild green chilies, drained
½ cup ⅓-less-salt chicken broth
½ teaspoon ground cumin
1 teaspoon dried oregano leaves, crushed
2 tablespoons chopped fresh cilantro (optional)

1 Place tomatillos in large saucepan; cover with water. Bring to a boil over high heat. Reduce heat to medium-high and simmer gently 20 to 30 minutes or until tomatillos are tender.

2 Place tomatillos, chilies, broth (omit if using canned tomatillos), cumin and oregano in food processor or blender; process until smooth. Return mixture to pan. Cover; heat over medium heat until bubbling. Stir in cilantro, if desired.

Makes about 3 cups

❖
Health Note
Herbs are a good way to add flavor to foods without adding calories, sodium or fat. This recipe combines oregano, cumin and fresh cilantro to pack it full of flavor.
❖

BREAKFAST BURRITOS WITH BAKED CITRUS FRUIT

❖

Fresh cilantro, also called corriander or Chinese parsley, is used extensively in Mexican cooking. This pungent herb is similar in appearance to flat-leaf parsley. It adds a distinct flavor to this dish, pictured on page 65.

❖

Nutrients per serving:

includes Baked Citrus Fruit

Calories	248
(16% of calories from fat)	
Total Fat	4 g
Saturated Fat	1 g
Cholesterol	11 mg
Sodium	218 mg
Carbohydrate	37 g
Dietary Fiber	5 g
Protein	16 g
Calcium	272 mg
Iron	3 mg
Vitamin A	499 RE
Vitamin C	109 mg

DIETARY EXCHANGES:
1¹⁄₂ Starch/Bread,
1¹⁄₂ Lean Meat, 1 Fruit

Nonstick cooking spray
4 green onions, thinly sliced, divided
1¹⁄₄ cups frozen egg substitute, thawed
2 tablespoons diced mild green chilies
¹⁄₂ cup (2 ounces) shredded reduced fat Monterey Jack *or* Cheddar cheese
¹⁄₄ cup lightly packed fresh cilantro
4 (7-inch) flour tortillas
¹⁄₄ cup Salsa Cruda (page 14)
¹⁄₄ cup low fat sour cream
    Baked Citrus Fruit (page 64)

1 Spray large nonstick skillet with cooking spray. Heat over medium heat. Set aside ¹⁄₄ cup green onions. Add remaining onions, egg substitute and chilies. Cook, stirring occasionally, about 4 minutes or until eggs are softly set. Stir in cheese and cilantro. Continue cooking, folding eggs over until eggs are cooked to desired doneness, about 1 minute.

2 Stack tortillas and wrap in paper towels. Microwave at HIGH (100% power) about 1 minute or until hot.

3 Place one-quarter of eggs in center of each tortilla. Fold sides over filling to enclose. Place burritos seam side down on plates. Top each with Salsa Cruda, 1 tablespoon low fat sour cream and reserved green onions. Serve with Baked Citrus Fruit.

Makes 4 servings

(continued on page 64)

Breakfast Burritos with Baked Citrus Fruit, continued

BAKED CITRUS FRUIT

> 2 oranges, peeled, sliced
> 1 grapefruit, peeled, sliced
> 1½ tablespoons lightly packed brown sugar
> ½ teaspoon ground cinnamon

1 Preheat oven to 400°F.

2 Divide fruit slices into 4 portions. Arrange each portion on baking sheet, overlapping slices.

3 Combine brown sugar and cinnamon in small bowl. Sprinkle 2 teaspoons mixture over each serving of fruit. Bake 5 minutes or until fruit is hot.   *Makes 4 servings*

❖

Health Note

Check labels on egg substitutes to know what you are buying. Some contain no fat or cholesterol and others simply reduce the levels found in fresh eggs.

❖

Main Dishes

BROILED CHICKEN BREAST WITH CILANTRO SALSA

❖

Skinless white meat of poultry has the lowest fat content of all meats, with only 25% of calories coming from fat. To keep it light, use dry heat cooking methods like broiling or grilling.

❖

Nutrients per serving:

Calories	122
(19% of calories from fat)	
Total Fat	3 g
Saturated Fat	1 g
Cholesterol	58 mg
Sodium	80 mg
Carbohydrate	2 g
Dietary Fiber	1 g
Protein	22 g
Calcium	26 mg
Iron	1 mg
Vitamin A	79 RE
Vitamin C	15 mg

DIETARY EXCHANGES:
3 Lean Meat, 1 Vegetable

4 small boneless skinless chicken breast halves (4 ounces each)
4 tablespoons lime juice, divided
   Black pepper
2 tablespoons pine nuts (optional)
½ cup lightly packed fresh cilantro, chopped
⅓ cup thinly sliced or minced green onions
¼ to ½ jalapeño pepper, seeded, minced

1 Spray broiler pan or baking sheet with nonstick cooking spray.

2 Brush chicken with 2 tablespoons lime juice. Place on prepared pan. Sprinkle generously with pepper; set aside.

3 To make Cilantro Salsa, heat large nonstick skillet over medium heat. Add pine nuts. Cook and stir 6 to 8 minutes or until golden. Combine remaining 2 tablespoons lime juice, pine nuts, cilantro, onions and jalapeño in small bowl; stir to combine. Set aside.

4 Broil chicken 1 to 2 inches from heat 8 to 10 minutes or until chicken is no longer pink in center. Serve with Cilantro Salsa. Garnish with lime slices, if desired.

Makes 4 servings

GRILLED SWORDFISH WITH PINEAPPLE SALSA

❖

One serving or more of seafood each week is linked with a lower risk of heart disease. All seafood is low in saturated fat and most is low in cholesterol.

❖

Nutrients per serving:

Calories	194
(28% of calories from fat)	
Total Fat	6 g
Saturated Fat	2 g
Cholesterol	56 mg
Sodium	183 mg
Carbohydrate	6 g
Dietary Fiber	1 g
Protein	28 g
Calcium	16 mg
Iron	2 mg
Vitamin A	76 RE
Vitamin C	20 mg

DIETARY EXCHANGES:
3 Lean Meat, ½ Fruit

1 tablespoon lime juice
2 cloves garlic, minced
4 swordfish steaks (5 ounces each)
½ teaspoon chili powder *or* coarse ground black pepper
   Pineapple Salsa (recipe follows)

1 Combine lime juice and garlic on plate. Dip swordfish in juice; sprinkle with chili powder.

2 Spray cold grid with nonstick cooking spray. Adjust grid 4 to 6 inches above heat. Preheat grill to medium-high heat. Grill fish, covered, 2 to 3 minutes. Turn over; grill 1 to 2 minutes more or until just opaque in center and still very moist. Top each serving with about 3 tablespoons Pineapple Salsa. *Makes 4 servings*

PINEAPPLE SALSA

½ cup finely chopped fresh pineapple
¼ cup finely chopped red bell pepper
1 green onion, thinly sliced
2 tablespoons lime juice
½ jalapeño pepper, seeded, minced
1 tablespoon chopped fresh cilantro *or* fresh basil

1 Combine all ingredients in small nonmetallic bowl; stir to combine. Serve at room temperature. *Makes 4 servings*

CHILE VERDE

½ to ¾ pound boneless lean pork
1 large onion, halved, thinly sliced
4 cloves garlic, chopped or sliced
1 pound fresh tomatillos
1 can (14½ ounces) ⅓-less-salt chicken broth
1 can (4 ounces) diced mild green chilies
1 teaspoon ground cumin
1½ cups cooked navy *or* Great Northern beans, *or* 1 can (15 ounces) Great Northern beans, rinsed and drained
½ cup lightly packed fresh cilantro, chopped
    Nonfat plain yogurt (optional)

1 Trim fat from pork; discard. Cut meat into ¾- to 1-inch cubes. Place pork, onion, garlic and ½ cup water into large saucepan. Cover; simmer over medium-low heat, stirring occasionally, 30 minutes (add more water if necessary). Uncover; boil over medium-high heat until liquid evaporates and meat browns.

2 Add tomatillos and broth; stir. Cover; simmer over medium heat 20 minutes or until tomatillos are tender. Tear tomatillos apart with 2 forks. Add chilies and cumin. Cover; simmer over medium-low heat 45 minutes or until meat is tender and tears apart easily (add more water or broth to keep liquid level the same). Add beans; simmer 10 minutes or until heated through. Stir in cilantro. Serve with yogurt, if desired.

Makes 4 servings

Nutrients per serving:	
Calories	311
(14% of calories from fat)	
Total Fat	5 g
Saturated Fat	1 g
Cholesterol	40 mg
Sodium	51 mg
Carbohydrate	42 g
Dietary Fiber	6 g
Protein	26 g
Calcium	89 mg
Iron	4 mg
Vitamin A	51 RE
Vitamin C	56 mg

DIETARY EXCHANGES:
1 Starch/Bread, 2 Lean Meat, ½ Vegetable

GARLIC CLAMS

2 pounds littleneck clams
2 teaspoons olive oil
2 tablespoons finely chopped onion
2 tablespoons chopped garlic
¼ cup chopped red bell pepper
½ cup dry white wine
2 tablespoons lemon juice
1 tablespoon chopped fresh parsley

1 Discard any clams that remain open when tapped with fingers. To clean clams, scrub with stiff brush under cold running water. Soak clams in mixture of ½ cup salt to 1 gallon water 20 minutes. Drain water; repeat 2 more times.

2 Heat oil over medium-high heat in large saucepan. Add onion and garlic; cook and stir about 3 minutes or until garlic is tender but not brown. Add pepper, wine, lemon juice and clams. Cover and simmer 3 to 10 minutes or until clams open. Transfer clams as they open to large bowl, covering to keep warm. Discard any clams that do not open. Increase heat to high. Add parsley; boil until liquid reduces to ¼ to ⅓ cup. Pour over clams; serve immediately. Garnish with parsley sprigs, if desired.

Makes 4 servings

❖

Clams are high in protein and an excellent source of calcium and iron.

❖

Nutrients per serving:

Calories	107
(25% of calories from fat)	
Total Fat	3 g
Saturated Fat	<1 g
Cholesterol	25 mg
Sodium	44 mg
Carbohydrate	5 g
Dietary Fiber	<1 g
Protein	10 g
Calcium	48 mg
Iron	10 mg
Vitamin A	77 RE
Vitamin C	24 mg

DIETARY EXCHANGES:
1 Lean Meat, 1 Vegetable,
½ Fat

❖

Cook's Tip
Clams can be cooked in a variety of ways, such as steaming and baking.
All clams should be cooked gently to prevent toughening.

❖

TURKEY MOLE

Rich mixtures of ground chilies, spices, nuts and seeds—moles (MO-lays) of endless variety are a specialty of southern Mexico. Some, like this one, even include a bit of chocolate.

❖

2½ pounds turkey legs *or* 3½ pounds chicken thighs
¼ cup sliced or slivered almonds, *or* unsalted roasted peanuts
2 tablespoons sesame seeds
   Mole Sauce (page 76)
¼ to ½ teaspoon sugar (optional)
¼ cup chopped fresh cilantro
3 cups cooked rice

1 Place turkey legs in stockpot or Dutch oven; cover with water. Bring to a boil over high heat. Reduce heat to medium. Cover; simmer 1½ hours or until meat is tender (cook chicken thighs 45 minutes); drain. Cool slightly. Remove skin, bones and fat; discard. Cut turkey into large cubes.

2 Heat large nonstick skillet over medium heat. Add almonds. Cook, stirring often, 4 to 5 minutes or until golden. Transfer almonds to small bowl. Add sesame seeds to skillet. Cook and stir 4 to 5 minutes or until golden. Set 2 teaspoons aside for garnish; add remaining sesame seeds to almonds. Reserve for Mole Sauce.

3 Prepare Mole Sauce.

4 Combine turkey and Mole Sauce in large nonstick skillet. Bring to a simmer over medium-high heat. Cover and simmer 10 minutes or until turkey is hot. Add water or additional broth if too thick; simmer uncovered if thin. Add sugar, if desired. Sprinkle with reserved sesame seeds and cilantro. Serve over rice. Garnish as desired.

Makes 8 servings

Nutrients per serving:

includes Mole Sauce

Calories	332
(32% of calories from fat)	
Total Fat	12 g
Saturated Fat	3 g
Cholesterol	57 mg
Sodium	110 mg
Carbohydrate	34 g
Dietary Fiber	3 g
Protein	24 g
Calcium	76 mg
Iron	4 mg
Vitamin A	153 RE
Vitamin C	8 mg

DIETARY EXCHANGES:
1½ Starch/Bread, 2½ Lean Meat, 1 Vegetable, ½ Fruit, 1 Fat

(continued on page 76)

Turkey Mole, continued

MOLE SAUCE

- 1 tablespoon olive oil
- 1 small onion, chopped
- ¼ cup chili powder
- 4 cloves garlic, minced
- 1 teaspoon ground cinnamon
- ½ teaspoon ground cloves
- ½ teaspoon anise seeds *or* fennel seeds
- 1 large tomato, seeded, chopped
- ⅓ cup raisins
- 1 large ripe banana, cut into 1-inch pieces
- 1 corn *or* flour tortilla, torn into pieces, *or* 1 slice bread, torn into pieces
- 2 cups ⅓-less-salt chicken broth, divided
- 1 square (1 ounce) semisweet chocolate

1 Heat oil over medium heat in large nonstick skillet. Add onion. Cook and stir 5 minutes or until tender. Add chili powder, garlic, cinnamon, cloves and anise seeds. Cook and stir 3 minutes or until mixture is dry and somewhat darker. Add tomato and raisins. Cover; cook 3 minutes or until tomato is tender.

2 Pour mixture into food processor with reserved almond mixture. Add banana, tortilla and ½ cup broth; process until puréed. Return to skillet over medium heat and bring to a simmer. Add chocolate; stir until melted. Add remaining 1½ cups broth; reduce heat to low. Cover; simmer 20 minutes, stirring occasionally, to allow flavors to blend.   *Makes about 3 cups*

PEPPER-SPICED BEEF SKEWERS AND BEANS

❖

Beef is the meat of choice in Northern Mexico, often cooked over an open grill. Using a small portion of meat intermixed with colorful vegetables, these skewers (pictured on page 79) look ample. Beans are a satisfying high fiber, low fat side dish sharing the same lively seasoning.

❖

Nutrients per serving:	
Calories	263
(19% of calories from fat)	
Total Fat	6 g
Saturated Fat	2 g
Cholesterol	27 mg
Sodium	41 mg
Carbohydrate	37 g
Dietary Fiber	7 g
Protein	19 g
Calcium	103 mg
Iron	5 mg
Vitamin A	125 RE
Vitamin C	62 mg

DIETARY EXCHANGES:
1½ Starch/Bread, 2 Lean Meat, 2 Vegetable

1½ pounds tender, lean beef such as tenderloin
1 large red bell pepper
1 large green bell pepper
1 large onion, halved
   Pepper-Spice Seasoning (page 78)
2 tablespoons lemon juice
2 teaspoons olive oil
3 cups cooked, drained, Great Northern, navy or pinto beans, *or* 2 cans (16 ounces each) beans, rinsed, drained
1 can (28 ounces) no-salt-added stewed tomatoes, drained
2 tablespoons firmly packed brown sugar
2 tablespoons chopped fresh parsley

1 Cut beef into ¾- to 1-inch cubes. Cut peppers and half of onion into ¾- to 1-inch squares (you will need 24 to 30 squares of each). Thread peppers and vegetables alternately onto 6 (10- to 12-inch) metal skewers beginning with 1 piece of each vegetable followed by 1 cube meat. Combine 2 tablespoons Pepper-Spice Seasoning with lemon juice in small bowl. Brush mixture over beef cubes.

2 Spray cold grid with nonstick cooking spray. Adjust grid 4 to 6 inches above heat. Preheat grill to medium-high heat. Grill skewers 8 to 10 minutes, turning every 2 to 3 minutes, or until meat is grilled to desired doneness.

3 Meanwhile, finely chop remaining onion half. Heat oil in medium saucepan over medium-high heat. Add onion and remaining 2 tablespoons spice mixture. Cook and stir 3 minutes or until onion is tender (do not let spices burn). Stir in beans, tomatoes and brown sugar. Cover; cook and stir until heated through. Stir in parsley.

Makes 6 servings

(continued on page 78)

Pepper Spiced Beef Skewers and Beans, continued

PEPPER–SPICE SEASONING

2 tablespoons lemon juice
2 tablespoons pressed or minced garlic
2 teaspoons dried oregano leaves, crushed
2 teaspoons black pepper
1 teaspoon ground cumin
1 teaspoon ground allspice

1 Combine all ingredients in small bowl; stir to combine.   *Makes 6 servings*

❖

Health Note

As a good source of protein and fiber, beans are hard to beat. There are about 5 grams of protein and almost 6 grams of fiber in a $1/3$-cup portion of beans. What is more, they have no cholesterol and only a trace of fat.

❖

BAKED ROCKFISH VERACRUZ

❖

Smothered with tomatoes and jalapeños from the New World, and capers and olives from the Old World, this fish dish offers omega-3 fatty acids (believed to help reduce cholesterol levels in the body), lots of vitamin C and very few calories.

❖

1 teaspoon olive oil
½ small onion, chopped
4 cloves garlic, minced
8 to 10 ounces ripe tomatoes, cored and chopped *or* 2 cans (15 ounces each) no-salt-added whole tomatoes, drained, chopped
½ green bell pepper, chopped
½ to 1 jalapeño pepper, seeded, minced (optional)
1 teaspoon dried oregano leaves, crushed
½ teaspoon ground cumin
¼ cup small pimiento-stuffed green olives
2 teaspoons drained capers (optional)
1 pound skinless rockfish, snapper, halibut or cod fillets

1 Preheat oven to 375°F.

2 Heat large nonstick skillet over medium-high heat. Add oil, onion and garlic. Cook and stir 3 minutes or until onion is tender. Add tomatoes, bell pepper, jalapeño, oregano and cumin. Cook over high heat, stirring occasionally, 2 to 3 minutes more. Stir in olives and capers, if desired; set aside.

3 Spray 11×7-inch baking pan with nonstick cooking spray. Place fish in single layer in pan, folding thin tail sections under to make fish evenly thick. Pour tomato mixture over fish. Cover with foil; bake 10 minutes or until fish is opaque and flakes easily when tested with fork. Serve with rice and garnish with fresh herbs, if desired.

Makes 4 servings

Nutrients per serving:

Calories	153
(26% of calories from fat)	
Total Fat	4 g
Saturated Fat	1 g
Cholesterol	39 mg
Sodium	347 mg
Carbohydrate	6 g
Dietary Fiber	2 g
Protein	22 g
Calcium	37 mg
Iron	1 mg
Vitamin A	108 RE
Vitamin C	22 mg

DIETARY EXCHANGES:
2½ Lean Meat,
1 Vegetable

LAMB & GREEN CHILE STEW

❖

Stew, in one form or another, is a basic dish worldwide. The combination of meats, fruits, vegetables and often grains offers a nearly perfect balance of nutrients—all from only one pot.

❖

1 pound boneless lean lamb, cubed
1 large onion, halved, sliced
6 cloves garlic, chopped or sliced
2 cans (15 ounces each) no-salt-added whole tomatoes, undrained
1 pound potatoes
3 cans (4 ounces each) diced mild green chilies
2 teaspoons dried rosemary leaves, crushed
1 teaspoon dried oregano leaves, crushed
1 pound zucchini
1 cup frozen whole kernel corn, thawed, drained
  Black pepper to taste
  Pickled jalapeño peppers (optional)

1 Combine ½ cup water, lamb, onion and garlic in large saucepan. Bring to a simmer over medium-high heat. Cover; simmer 30 minutes or until onion is tender. Increase heat to high; uncover. Boil, stirring occasionally, until liquid evaporates and browns. Add tomatoes with liquid; stir. Reduce heat to medium-low. Cover; simmer 30 minutes.

2 Meanwhile, cut potatoes into 1½-inch pieces. Add potatoes, chilies, rosemary and oregano. Cover; simmer 20 to 30 minutes or until potatoes and lamb are tender.

3 Halve zucchini lengthwise and cut crosswise into ½- to ¾-inch pieces. Add zucchini and corn to stew. Cover; simmer 10 minutes or until zucchini is crisp-tender. Season with black pepper. Garnish with jalapeños, if desired.   *Makes 6 servings*

Nutrients per serving:

Calories   246
(15% of calories from fat)
Total Fat   4 g
Saturated Fat   1 g
Cholesterol   38 mg
Sodium   58 mg
Carbohydrate   37 g
Dietary Fiber   6 g
Protein   18 g
Calcium   85 mg
Iron   4 mg
Vitamin A   126 RE
Vitamin C   123 mg

DIETARY EXCHANGES:
1½ Starch/Bread, 1½ Lean Meat, 2½ Vegetable

CHICKEN SCALOPPINE WITH LEMON-CAPER SAUCE

Healthy eating requires healthy cooking techniques. To minimize the oil normally used to pan-fry scaloppine, use a well seasoned or heavy-bottomed pan and spray it with nonstick cooking spray before heating.

1 pound boneless skinless chicken breasts
3 tablespoons all-purpose flour, divided
¼ teaspoon black pepper
¼ teaspoon chili powder
½ cup ⅓-less-salt chicken broth
1 tablespoon lemon juice
1 tablespoon drained capers
½ teaspoon olive oil

1 Place chicken breasts, 1 at a time, between sheets of waxed paper. Pound to ¼ inch thickness. Combine 2 tablespoons flour, pepper and chili powder in shallow plate. Dip chicken pieces in flour mixture to lightly coat both sides.

2 Combine broth, lemon juice, remaining tablespoon flour and capers in small bowl.

3 Spray large skillet with nonstick cooking spray; heat over medium-high heat. Place chicken in hot pan in single layer; cook 1½ minutes. Turn over; cook 1 to 1½ minutes or until chicken is no longer pink in center. Repeat with remaining chicken (brush pan with ¼ teaspoon oil each time you add pieces to prevent sticking). If cooking more than 2 batches, reduce heat to medium to prevent burning chicken.

4 Pour broth mixture into skillet. Boil, uncovered, until thickened and reduced to about ¼ cup. Serve immediately over chicken. *Makes 4 servings*

Nutrients per serving:

Calories 144
(26% of calories from fat)
Total Fat 4 g
Saturated Fat 1 g
Cholesterol 58 mg
Sodium 67 mg
Carbohydrate 4 g
Dietary Fiber <1 g
Protein 22 g
Calcium 13 mg
Iron 1 mg
Vitamin A 22 RE
Vitamin C 2 mg

DIETARY EXCHANGES:
2½ Lean Meat

STUFFED BELL PEPPERS

❖

*Peppers are a rich source
of vitamin C and the
perfect vessel for this mild
corn filling.*

❖

1 package (8½ ounces) cornbread mix *plus* ingredients for preparation
6 green bell peppers
1 large onion, thinly sliced
1 teaspoon olive oil
1 can (16 ounces) no-salt-added diced tomatoes
1 package (10 ounces) frozen whole kernel corn, thawed, drained
1 can (2¼ ounces) sliced ripe olives, drained
⅓ cup raisins
1 tablespoon chili powder
1 teaspoon ground sage
1 cup (4 ounces) shredded reduced fat Monterey Jack cheese, divided

1 Prepare cornbread according to package directions. Cut into cubes. *Reduce oven temperature to 350°F.*

2 Slice tops off peppers. Discard stems and seeds. Finely chop tops to equal 1 cup; set aside. Rinse peppers. Bring 2 to 3 inches water to a boil over high heat in large saucepan. Add 1 or more peppers and boil 1 minute, turning peppers with tongs to blanch evenly. Rinse with cold water; drain. Repeat with remaining peppers.

3 Place onion and oil in Dutch oven. Cover; cook over medium-high heat, stirring occasionally, 8 to 10 minutes or until onion is tender and browned. Add 1 to 2 tablespoons water, if needed, to prevent sticking. Add chopped pepper; stir 1 minute more. Remove from heat. Add tomatoes, corn, olives, raisins, chili powder and sage; stir. Stir in corn bread (it will crumble) and ¾ cup cheese.

4 Spoon filling into peppers. Top with remaining ¼ cup cheese. Place peppers in baking dish; bake 20 to 30 minutes or until heated through. Garnish with cherry tomato halves and fresh herbs, if desired.

Makes 6 servings